IT'S SO COLD IN WISCONSIN... ™

BY BONNIE STEWART
AND CATHY McGLYNN

BLUE SKY
MARKETING INC.

BLUE SKY MARKETING INC.
PO Box 21583-S St. Paul, MN 55121 USA

W0017615

It's So Cold™ In Wisconsin…
Copyright © 1997 by Bonnie Stewart and Cathy McGlynn
Design by Scott Drude
Edited by Vic Spadaccini

Cheesehead™ name and likeness Licensed by Foamation, Inc., Milwaukee, WI.
Packers® and Vikings® are registered trademarks of the Green Bay Packers Incorporated
and the Minnesota Vikings Football Club.

Printed in the United States of America
ISBN: 0-911493-20-4

Published by:
BLUE SKY MARKETING INC.
PO Box 21583-S
St. Paul, MN 55121 USA
(651) 456-5602 [new area code eff. 7/1/98] / 800-444-5450
SAN 263-9394

8   7   6   5   4   3

DEDICATED TO:

All the hearty Wisconsinites, who bravely faced the elements during the record-breaking cold winter of '95-96. You, along with the weather, were indeed our inspiration!

P.S. Thanks to El Niño, the winter of '97-98 was warmer than most – people were wearing shorts at 45°F above zero. What will future winters bring?

IT'S SO COLD IN WISCONSIN....

WHEN YOU INHALE,
YOUR NOSTRILS STICK TOGETHER!

IT'S SO COLD
IN WISCONSIN...

PEOPLE USE TWO SETS OF KEYS
SO THEY DON'T HAVE TO TURN OFF THE CAR
WHILE SHOPPING

IT'S SO COLD IN WISCONSIN....

YOU WOULD RATHER GET A PARKING TICKET
THAN GO OUT TO PLUG THE METER

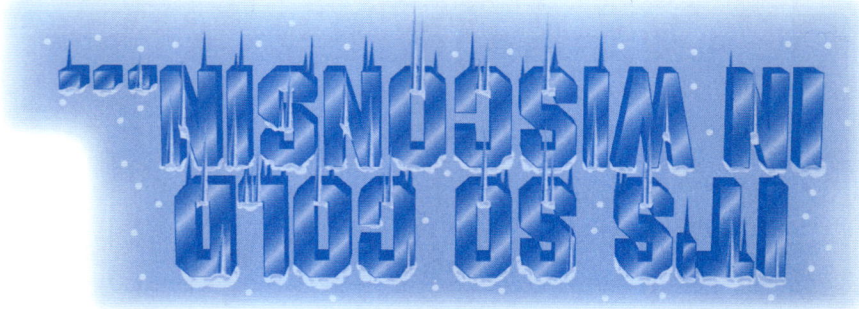

"IT'S SO COLD IN WISCONSIN..."

A 'CONGA LINE' REFERS TO A FORMATION OF SNOW PLOWS, NOT A LATIN DANCE

IT'S SO COLD IN WISCONSIN...

WHEN YOU COME IN FROM OUTSIDE, YOUR GLASSES FOG UP SO BAD YOU CAN'T SEE!

IF THE STATUE OF LIBERTY WAS IN
THE SUPERIOR HARBOR, SHE WOULD HAVE HER
TORCH UNDER HER DRESS.

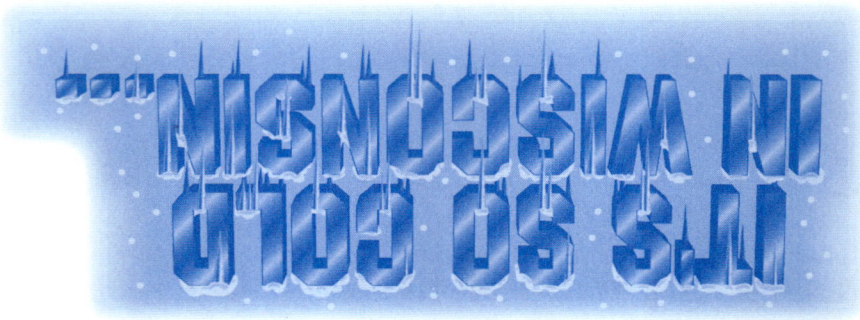

"IT'S SO COLD IN WISCONSIN"

IT'S SO COLD
IN WISCONSIN...

SEVERAL PEOPLE DROWN EVERY YEAR ATTEMPTING
TO DIG BASEMENTS FOR THEIR
ICE FISHING HOUSES

IT'S SO COLD IN WISCONSIN...

WHEN YOU BLOW BUBBLES, THEY FREEZE AND YOU CAN PICK THEM UP

IT'S SO COLD IN WISCONSIN...

KNOBS ON CAR RADIOS DON'T TURN BECAUSE THEY'RE FROZEN

IT'S SO COLD
IN WISCONSIN...

PEOPLE CAN'T TELL IF YOUR SPEECH IS SLURRED
FROM DRINKING OR BECAUSE YOUR FACE
IS NUMB

IT'S SO COLD IN WISCONSIN...

YOU THINK YOU KICKED A ROCK ON THE
SIDEWALK AND THEN REALIZE IT'S DOG-DOO!

IT'S SO COLD
IN WISCONSIN...

YOU DON'T HAVE TO BE JESUS
TO WALK ON WATER

IT'S SO COLD IN WISCONSIN...

THAT PEOPLE DON'T LOOK TWICE IF A MAN WALKS INTO A BANK WEARING A SKI MASK

IT'S SO COLD
IN WISCONSIN...

YOUR DOORS FREEZE AND YOU CAN'T
GET IN YOUR CAR

IT'S SO COLD IN WISCONSIN....

YOUR DOORS FREEZE AND YOU CAN'T GET <u>OUT</u> OF YOUR CAR

IT'S SO COLD IN WISCONSIN...

MEN WALK AROUND WITH ICICLES HANGING FROM THEIR BEARDS

IT'S SO COLD IN WISCONSIN...

CHILDREN WEAR SO MANY LAYERS OF CLOTHING
THAT THEY CAN'T GET UP IF THEY FALL DOWN

IT'S SO COLD
IN WISCONSIN....

YOUR CAR FINALLY STARTS BLOWING WARM AIR
JUST AS YOU PULL INTO
THE PARKING LOT AT WORK

IT'S SO COLD IN WISCONSIN....

PACKER® FANS ARE NOW TOUGHER THAN VIKINGS® FANS

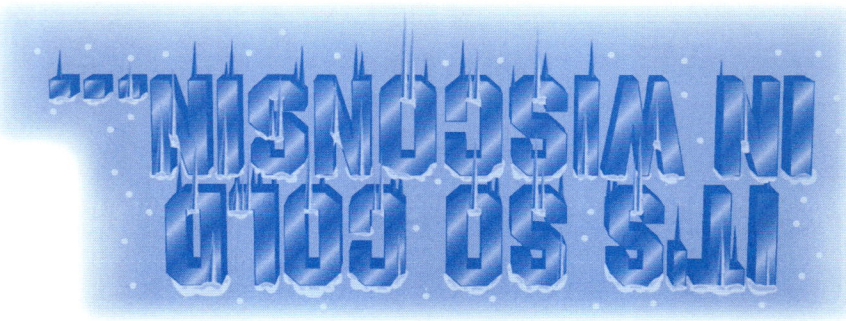

PEOPLE PAY EXTRA FOR WARM BEER

"...IT'S SO COLD IN WISCONSIN..."

THERE ARE 'BLACK ICE' WARNINGS

(WHEN THE MOISTURE FROM CAR EXHAUST FREEZES ON THE PAVEMENT)

THE #1 EXCUSE FOR NOT GOING TO WORK IS
"IT'S TOO DARN COLD!"

IT'S SO COLD IN WISCONSIN....

THE #2 EXCUSE FOR NOT GOING TO WORK IS
"I FORGOT TO PLUG IN MY CAR"

IT'S SO COLD
IN WISCONSIN...

COWS AUTOMATICALLY PRODUCE SOFT
SERVE ICE CREAM

IT'S SO COLD IN WISCONSIN...

WHEN YOU SEE THE MORNING TEMPERATURE IS -28º F YOU'RE HAPPY, BECAUSE IT'S GOING TO BE A NICE DAY!

IT'S SO COLD
IN WISCONSIN...

FROSTY THE SNOWMAN ASKS
TO COME IN THE HOUSE!

IT'S SO COLD IN WISCONSIN...

YOU CAN POUND NAILS WITH A FROZEN BANANA!

IT'S SO COLD IN WISCONSIN...

INSTRUCTORS CONSIDER HOLDING SPRING
CANOE LESSONS IN INDOOR SWIMMING POOLS

WE HAVE NINE MONTHS OF WINTER AND
THREE MONTHS OF TOUGH SLEDDING

IT'S SO COLD IN WISCONSIN...

IT KEEPS THE RIFF RAFF OUT

IT'S SO COLD
IN WISCONSIN...

THE BIGGEST ACCOMPLISHMENT OF THE DAY IS
GETTING YOUR CAR STARTED!

IT'S SO COLD IN WISCONSIN...

RADIO STATIONS AND BARS HOLD CONTESTS TO
SEE WHO CAN BEST IMITATE THE SOUND OF A CAR
TRYING TO START

IT'S SO COLD IN WISCONSIN...

THAT FOR FUN, WE THROW CUPS OF HOT WATER OUT OUR BACK DOORS TO WATCH IT CRYSTALLIZE IN MIDAIR

IT'S SO COLD IN WISCONSIN...

PEOPLE MIGRATE SOUTH FOR THE WINTER
JUST LIKE MANY BIRDS
(WE EVEN HAVE A NAME FOR THEM - 'SNOWBIRDS')

IT'S SO COLD IN WISCONSIN...

ABANDONED OR SNOWED IN CARS ARE NICKNAMED 'SNOWBIRDS' (ALTERNATE DEFINITION)

THE #1 GREETING IS "COLD ENOUGH FOR YA?"

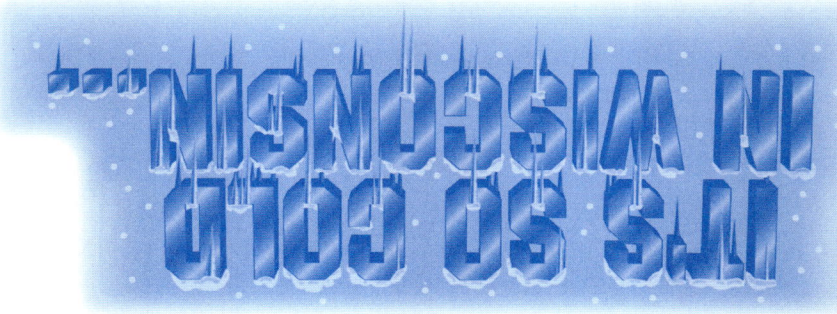

"IT'S SO COLD IN WISCONSIN..."

IT'S SO COLD IN WISCONSIN...

THE #2 SAYING IS "I CAN'T WAIT UNTIL THOSE DARN MOSQUITOES GET HERE, AT LEAST IT'LL BE WARM!"

(IN SUMMER, THE #2 SAYING IS "I CAN'T WAIT UNTIL WINTER, AT LEAST THERE WON'T BE ANY DARN MOSQUITOES!")

IT'S SO COLD IN WISCONSIN...

THEY SOMETIMES HAVE TO CANCEL WINTER SURVIVAL CLASSES!

THEY CANCEL SCHOOL AND EVEN FUNERALS!

IT'S SO COLD
IN WISCONSIN....

WE SOMETIMES HAVE TO CALL OUR NEIGHBORS TO
SHOVEL THE SNOW AWAY FROM THE DOOR SO WE
CAN GET <u>OUT</u> OF THE HOUSE!

IT'S SO COLD IN WISCONSIN....

THE #1 RESPONSE TO "HOW ARE YOU?" IS "COLD!"

WHEN YOU SIT ON A TOILET, THE SEAT IS SO COLD YOU DECIDE TO WAIT

IT'S SO COLD IN WISCONSIN...

INSTEAD OF SMOG WARNINGS, THERE ARE WIND CHILL WARNINGS!

(SOME WARNINGS EXCEED 90° BELOW ZERO F)

IT'S SO COLD
IN WISCONSIN....

WE SAW A STREAKER
AND HE WAS FROZEN IN PLACE!

IT'S SO COLD IN WISCONSIN....

WHEN YOU'RE ICE FISHING, YOU CAN HEAR THE FISH SHIVERING!

IT'S SO COLD IN WISCONSIN....

PEOPLE WEAR LONG JOHNS UNDER BUSINESS SUITS

IT'S SO COLD
IN WISCONSIN...

WISCONSINITES SAY TO EACH OTHER,
"IT'S ◎?✳! COLD OUT!" BUT TO A NON-WISCONSINITE
THEY'LL SAY "YUP, IT'S A LITTLE CHILLY TODAY"

IT'S SO COLD IN WISCONSIN...

IT'S A STATUS SYMBOL TO HAVE ARCTIC
EXPEDITION RATED BOOTS

IT'S SO COLD
IN WISCONSIN...

WE 'GRILL' OUR CAR ENGINES WITH CHARCOAL
BRIQUETTES TO WARM THEM UP!

IT'S SO COLD IN WISCONSIN...

DAILY ACTIVITIES ALWAYS "DEPEND ON THE WEATHER"

IT'S SO COLD IN WISCONSIN...

THAT PEOPLE USE HOCKEY STICKS TO FIRE FROZEN DOG DOO INTO THEIR NEIGHBORS' YARDS

IT'S SO COLD
IN WISCONSIN....

HOUSES ACTUALLY CREAK, SNAP, AND POP
IN THE NIGHT

ON MEN'S NIGHT OUT, THE GUYS STAY HOME

IT'S SO COLD
IN WISCONSIN...

EVEN SENSUOUS WOMEN
WEAR WOOL SOCKS TO BED!

IT'S SO COLD IN WISCONSIN....

WHEN IT WARMS UP TO -10° F
YOU CAN UNZIP YOUR COAT

IT'S SO COLD
IN WISCONSIN....

HOSPITALS REPORT
AN INCREASE IN BROKEN TOES, FROM PEOPLE
KICKING THE 'CHUNKS' OFF THEIR CARS

IT'S SO COLD IN WISCONSIN...

FROM NOVEMBER THROUGH MARCH, LADIES
NEVER SUFFER FROM HOT FLASHES!

IT HURTS YOUR TEETH TO INHALE
THROUGH YOUR MOUTH

IT'S SO COLD IN WISCONSIN...

THAT ALL FLIGHTS LEAVING THE AIRPORT
REFUSE TO COME BACK!

IT'S SO COLD
IN WISCONSIN...

YOU CAN'T WAIT TO GET INTO AN ICE ARENA
TO WARM UP

IT'S SO COLD
IN WISCONSIN...

EVEN THE ALBERTA CLIPPERS SWING SOUTH
(THIS IS A TERM FOR A COLD FRONT, NOT A GROUP OF BARBERS)

IT'S SO COLD IN WISCONSIN...

YOU GET OUT OF THE CAR TO CHECK THE TIRES... NOT BECAUSE YOU THINK THEY'RE FLAT, BUT BECAUSE YOU THINK THEY'RE SQUARE!

IT'S SO COLD IN WISCONSIN...

YOUR FIRST BREATH UPON GOING OUTSIDE IS MORE LIKE A GASP!

IT'S SO COLD IN WISCONSIN...

9 MONTHS AFTER A COLD SNAP OR BLIZZARD,
THE HOSPITALS ARE FULL OF NEW BABIES!

RUDOLPH'S NOSE GETS SO COLD IT TURNS BLUE!

THAT TOWNS COMPETE
TO SEE WHICH IS COLDER!
(THE CITY OF COUDERAY HOLDS THE RECORD OF -55° F IN 1996)

IT'S SO COLD IN WISCONSIN...

WHEN IT'S 40°F <u>ABOVE</u> ZERO, PEOPLE START WASHING THEIR CARS!

IT'S SO COLD
IN WISCONSIN...

FLASHERS WOULD RATHER JUST
DESCRIBE THEMSELVES

IT'S SO COLD IN WISCONSIN...

THERE ARE DOGS FROZEN TO FIRE HYDRANTS!

YOU HAVE ICE
ON BOTH SIDES OF YOUR WINDSHIELD

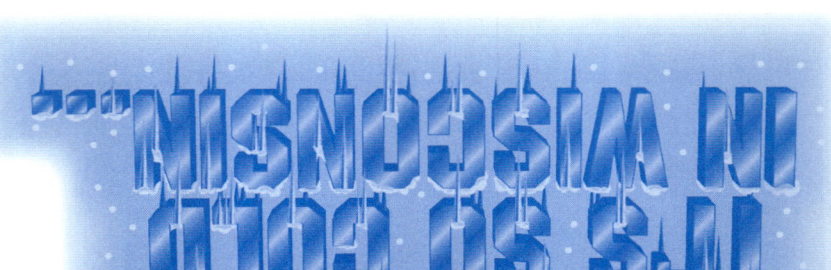

"...IT'S SO COLD IN WISCONSIN..."

IT'S SO COLD
IN WISCONSIN....

PEOPLE ARE TREATED FOR COLD BURNS RATHER
THAN SUNBURN!

THE #1 CHRISTMAS GIFT IS A CAR SURVIVAL KIT!

IT'S SO COLD IN WISCONSIN....

THERE IS NOTHING ELSE TO TALK ABOUT

IT'S SO COLD IN WISCONSIN...

THE GROUNDHOG DOESN'T COME OUT UNTIL
MAY TO SEE IF THERE ARE 6 WEEKS LEFT
OF WINTER

THAT PEOPLE WEAR ELECTRIC SOCKS

IT'S SO COLD IN WISCONSIN...

SHIVERING IS CONSIDERED A FORM OF AEROBICS

IT'S SO COLD IN WISCONSIN...

YOU CAN COUNT ON AN INCREASE IN BEEF PRICES BECAUSE BULLS GO STERILE (SOME REALLY DO!)

IT'S SO COLD
IN WISCONSIN...

THERE ARE HEATED BUS SHELTERS ON CITY
STREET CORNERS

IT'S SO COLD IN WISCONSIN....

SOME LAKE BOTTOMS DON'T THAW UNTIL THE MIDDLE OF JULY

(SOME SAY THE SAME THING ABOUT PEOPLE!)

IT'S SO COLD IN WISCONSIN...

WE HAVE ONLY TWO SEASONS - "WINTER" AND
"ROAD REPAIR"

IT'S SO COLD
IN WISCONSIN...

EVEN IOWA LOOKS GOOD!

IT'S SO COLD IN WISCONSIN...

PEOPLE TOW REAL HOUSES ONTO LAKES SO
THEY CAN FISH IN COMFORT

(SOME HAVE TWO AND THREE BEDROOMS!)

IT'S SO COLD IN WISCONSIN....

THERE IS A THRIVING HOUSE RENTAL
BUSINESS – FOR ICE FISHING HOUSES!

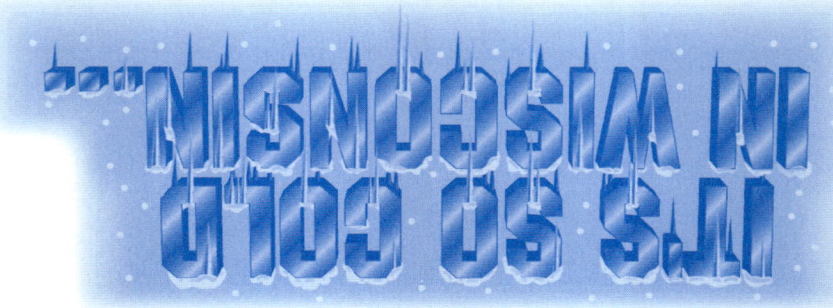

"IT'S SO COLD
IN WISCONSIN..."

AFTER MAKING LOVE, HUSBANDS ACTUALLY
WANT TO CUDDLE

IT'S SO COLD
IN WISCONSIN...

THAT LAWYERS WILL SOMETIMES PUT THEIR
HANDS IN THEIR OWN POCKETS

YOUR CHEESEHEAD™ FREEZES TO YOUR HEAD

YOUR GARAGE DOOR FREEZES SHUT AND YOU CAN'T GET IN (OR OUT!)

IT'S SO COLD
IN WISCONSIN...

THE SNOW SOUNDS LIKE YOU'RE WALKING
ON STYROFOAM

IT'S SO COLD IN WISCONSIN....

THAT YOUR DOCTOR PUTS ON <u>YOUR</u> CLOTHES
AFTER YOU TAKE THEM OFF

IT'S SO COLD IN WISCONSIN...

THE MOST POPULAR CULTURES ARE THROAT

OUR SINCERE THANKS TO THE FOLLOWING PEOPLE AND ORGANIZATIONS FOR THEIR CONTRIBUTIONS:

Bart Bender
Mark Bohrer
Gene & Adelle Carr
Dave Carr
Scott Drude

Ron Eberhardt
Steve Foss
Bruce Hagovik
Caroline Hanrahan
John Hogan
Matt Menne

Craig McKee
Don Peterson
Susan Schreifels
Kerri Spadaccini
Corinne Stefanson

AFTERWORD...

As we laughed ourselves through this book project, we felt fortunate that we were able to have warm shelter and hot meals to sustain us through some of the coldest days that we have experienced. We know there were many families not as fortunate. In our sincerest respect to those who may have felt the cold more deeply than most, we are donating a portion of the profits of this book to "Loaves and Fishes," the Fosston, Minnesota food shelf, a local organization that assists many families in our area throughout the year.

Finally, if you'd like to send us your own additions to this book, we'd like to read them. We may even use them in our next edition! Please send them to us care of our publisher: Blue Sky Marketing, PO Box 21583, St. Paul, MN 55121 USA. Note that all items submitted become the property of the publisher and no compensation or recognition will be given.